Spring Harvest Bible Workbook

Church

WHAT WE CAN LEARN FROM ACTS

BEKI ROGERS

First published in 2020

Essential Christian, 14 Horsted Square, Uckfield, TN22 1QG Tel: 01825 746530
Email: info@essentialchristian.org Web: essentialchristian.org
Registered charity number 1126997

IVP, 36 Causton Street, London SW1P 4ST, England
Email: ivp@ivpbooks.com Web: www.ivpbooks.com

ISBN: 978-1-78974-179-7
eBook ISBN: 978-1-78974-180-3

Typeset by Ascent Creative
Web: ascent-creative.co.uk

Printed and bound in Great Britain by
Ashford Colour Press Ltd, Gosport, Hampshire

Contents

Inter-Varsity Press publishes Christian books that are true to the Bible and that communicate the gospel, develop discipleship and strengthen the church for its mission in the world.

IVP originated within the Inter-Varsity Fellowship, now the Universities and Colleges Christian Fellowship, a student movement connecting Christian Unions in universities and colleges throughout Great Britain, and a member movement of the International Fellowship of Evangelical Students.
Website: www.uccf.org.uk. That historic association is maintained, and all senior IVP staff and committee members subscribe to the UCCF Basis of Faith.

Introduction

When the Church was formed in the book of Acts, it was designed to be unleashed on society to make God's kingdom known. When we look at these early stages of church life, it looks very exciting and inspiring. Thousands of people were coming to faith, there were signs and wonders of the kingdom happening daily, and there was a dynamic and exciting community all giving and living together for God's work. It was an exciting time. What we don't always see is the struggle with agreeing on theology, the tension in how things should be organized, and who should lead what. This early church needed to organize itself so that the work of Jesus could continue to grow.

Now 2000 years on, there is a danger that we play at being church rather than being unleashed to be the church. We can do this because we feel like we want to do it right or be in control, but the early church was a community who were filled with the Holy Spirit and from this, unleashed to simply be themselves and no one else. The Church is unleashed to do the work of God, living out the mission of God in every neighbourhood for every individual to meet with God. As the Church grew, they realized that to stay unleashed, they needed to set some structure. Structure wasn't the opposite of being unleashed but the framework for the people of God to stay unleashed. This process of structuring the community and being filled with a dynamic spirit requires walking a fine line, and one can easily fall either way. We can be so unleashed that no one knows what is going on, and we can be so structured that we get nothing done. The Church is to walk this fine line.

When we look at the Church, it can be useful to have a set of characteristics to consider as we work out how we compare to the early church and how we fulfil the mission that we have been given.

Dulles, a theologian, identified six different aspects or characteristics that the Church holds in tension as it seeks to work out its mission in the world. This Study Guide takes these six aspects and adds one extra, Power, and then looks at what they are and how they can be seen within the local church.

This study looks at those characteristics, examines where they are seen in Acts, looks at the strengths and weaknesses behind them and encourages the reader to look at their own church community and reflect on how it encounters its context and which aspect it needs to develop to fulfil its mission to the world.

It also encourages readers to look at how those characteristics are reflected in their own lives, challenging them to become more Christ-like in the process.

It is important to remember that each of our local churches is part of the worldwide Body of Christ. Some churches will have different emphases and different focuses. Some denominations consider some aspects more important than others – but it is as a whole that we reflect the kingdom of God, not as individuals.

I love the local church! I think it is a beautiful and wonderful thing. It is the Body of Christ, but made up of fallen and imperfect people like me and you. So it is not ideal and not perfect. My prayer is that this study can be a celebration of what your church does and an opportunity to grow and develop in the way that God is leading. Please don't allow it to be a general church-bashing exercise – this is Christ's beloved that we are considering!

The Church Unleashed as Family

 Introduction

For all of us the word *family* conjures up images and concepts, some very positive and for some very negative. But it is a phrase that has been used to describe church over the ages. It may be that this section is hard for some of us to engage with as our experiences of family or even people in church have caused hurt and pain. So be aware of the individuals within your group, and allow hurt to be acknowledged if it arises.

It's important to remember that when we describe the Church as family, we are not using the sickly sweet Hollywood image we often see portrayed around Christmas of the ideal nuclear family unit, with no conflict and perfect teeth. We are looking at the wider image of the Church as a group of individuals who come together under one Father. All through the story of the People of God in the Bible, there are families – good godly ones and very dysfunctional ones – but they all share their relationship to God the Creator.

This section is going to explore how the idea of Church can be unleashed as family to draw others into that relationship.

Way in

There are many different images of family and community within the media. Some are families that are related by blood, for example, the Simpsons, and others are communities that are created by strong friendship ties like the group on 'Big Bang Theory'.

Q: What are your favourite fictional or non-fictional families from TV, book or film and why?

Q: What connects them together or identifies them as a family?

We are often a part of many different organizations and communities that we impact and that have an impact on us.

Q: What types of organizations or groups of people have you belonged to?

Q: When/where have you felt a sense of belonging and community?

My thoughts and notes...

◗ Introduction to Family

The early Church was initially made up of a very close friendship group. They were the people who had spent time following Jesus very closely, had seen him die and encountered him when he rose again. The initial converts that joined them became part of that close community, sharing life and worshipping together.

Q: Briefly reflect on your church family and who is part of it.

Q: What other Christian communities are you part of or are you aware of? (e.g. online, religious communities, rules of life, organizations, charities)

When we look at the Bible, we find two ways of looking at the Church as family. The first is as the People of God, the second is that of the Body of Christ. Each image has a different emphasis.

The Body of Christ is an image that comes from Paul's letters to the Romans and Corinthians; this image compares the Church to a body, where all the members are different parts, all important and valued but with different and unique purposes. This image has an emphasis on mutual concern for all the members and mutual dependence on one another. All in the family are connected and are valued for their uniqueness but also dependent on one another. There is a very strong sense of belonging.

The other image is that of the People of God: A group of people travelling together and connected like a family, which draws its image from the Israelites. The people of Israel were initially a family and then a tribe or extended family who served to point the way to God.

Both images are used to depict the Church as a family or a community that exists to draw others round it to connect with Jesus.

Q: What are the positive things in your church community that link to church as family?

Q: How does the family of the Church allow others to join it?

Q: Are there aspects of your church family that make it harder for others to join, or that stop it from engaging in its mission?

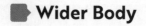

Wider Body

Read Acts 2:42–47

[42] They devoted themselves to the apostles' teaching and to fellowship, to the breaking of bread and to prayer. [43] Everyone was filled with awe at the many wonders and signs performed by the apostles. [44] All the believers were together and had everything in common. [45] They sold property and possessions to give to anyone who had need. [46] Every day they continued to meet together in the temple courts. They broke bread in their homes and ate together with glad and sincere hearts, [47] praising God and enjoying the favour of all the people. And the Lord added to their number daily those who were being saved.

Q: What strikes you about this passage?

Q: What questions do you have?

The early Church had an intense sense of family and community – of oneness, sharing, worshipping and being together. This passage gives us a wonderful idyllic image of the early Church. They are all pulling together, sharing and supporting one another. Many people look at this and long to experience the same level of belonging.

Q: What encourages you from the reading in your own engagement with church as family?

However, as we carry on reading Acts, we discover that there were disagreements as the Church worked out how to engage with the community around them and the mission that Jesus had left them (for example, in Acts 15). In fact, not much further on than the passage we looked at, we find individuals who were part of the early Church lying to the apostles by trying to pretend that what they were giving to the common purse was more significant than it actually was. We can see that there was conflict and deceit right at the beginning of the early Church. This is a very hard passage to look at and requires a more in-depth analysis to unpack it than is possible here[1]. But the important thing to register is that even in this early Church, there were problems.

The Church while being described as a family is by definition made up of individuals. One thing we know from the Bible is that as individuals none of us is perfect, we all have our own experiences, weaknesses and faults, which therefore impact on the whole.

---

1   See John Stott, *The Message of Acts* (IVP: Nottingham, 1992), and Tom Wright, *Acts for Everyone* (SPCK: London, 2008)

Q: How are you challenged and encouraged knowing that even the early Church had problems?

Response

Q: Where have you experienced the best of family within the Church?

Q: What are the things that prevent the Church from regularly living this out?

Parts of the Body

The theologian Dietrich Bonhoeffer says 'The community [family] is constituted by the complete self-forgetfulness of love. The relationship between I and thou is no longer essentially a demanding one but a giving one.'[2]

The idea of the Church as a perfect family is very attractive, especially in this day and age when so many people's experience of family is hurtful or non-existent. However it depends on the individuals working together to be 'giving' not demanding. High expectations!

Read Acts 15:36–41

[36] Some time later Paul said to Barnabas, "Let us go back and visit the believers in all the towns where we preached the word of the Lord and see how they are doing." [37] Barnabas wanted to take John, also called Mark, with them, [38] but Paul did not think it wise to take him, because he had deserted them in Pamphylia and had not continued with them in the work. [39] They had such a sharp disagreement that they parted company. Barnabas took Mark and sailed for Cyprus, [40] but Paul chose Silas and left, commended by the believers to the grace of the Lord. [41] He went through Syria and Cilicia, strengthening the churches.

Paul and Barnabas had been working together for the gospel for a long time, but in Acts 15 we read of a major disagreement that they had over Mark. Barnabas wanted to forgive him for his previous mistake of deserting them and to take him on the next journey with them; however, Paul disagreed. So the two went their separate ways and didn't go on the next journey together. This is just one example of disagreement within the early Church family.

In society today, there is disagreement over many

Dietrich Bonhoeffer, The Communion of Saints, quoted in Avery Dulles, Models of the Church, (Random House, New York: 2002), p.

things, from which is the best coffee to whether it is good for the country to have left the EU or not. Within the Church we are often faced with disagreements which can be theological or more practical (what coffee to serve). But how do we as a church community disagree well, so that we can show the world what it means to be part of the family of God?

In Matthew 5, Jesus gives us a wonderful image of trying to take a speck out of our neighbour's eye while ignoring the plank within our own. If you imagine what this might really look like, it is a humorous image, but so often we find noticing the mistakes and problems with those around us so much easier than acknowledging our own. This is something that can get in the way of us leaning into the family of the Church.

Response

Where is your family or community?

The early Church operated in three different levels of community:

- The temple courts - where a large group of people gathered publicly

- Their homes – where they gathered for fellowship and breaking bread together

- The wider community – the believers won the favour of all the people with their radical community living, at least until persecution began

Think about where you live out your faith within the three different family areas: The big family (their church community); the immediate family (their family and very close friends), and their wider community (their friendships, work relationships and connections).

Q: Who do you relate to in the different areas?

Q: How do you live out your faith within those communities?

Pray for the communities and other ways of drawing others into the Family of God.

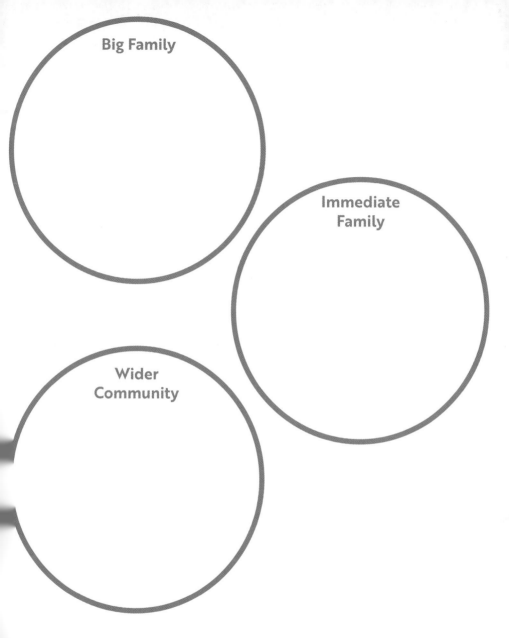

Big Family

Immediate Family

Wider Community

Prayer

Spend some time in silence acknowledging the times you have focused on specks that belong to others, and ask God to reveal the planks in your own eyes.

Then pray for opportunities to share your faith within your neighbourhood, both at the table and the marketplace.

The Church Unleashed as Servant

Introduction

The model that Jesus gave us was not just of one that preached the Good News, but also one that lived and demonstrated it. When Jesus came out of the wilderness and stood in the synagogue, he quoted Isaiah 61:1-2 when he said:

> The Spirit of the Sovereign Lord is on me,
>
> > because the Lord has anointed me
> >
> > to proclaim good news to the poor.
>
> He has sent me to bind up the broken-hearted,
>
> > to proclaim freedom for the captives
> >
> > and release from darkness for the prisoners,
>
> to proclaim the year of the Lord's favour.

During his ministry, Jesus did not only preach, he also demonstrated the words of Isaiah. He embodied the servant nature of the kingdom, including washing his disciples' feet.

The Church through the ages has acted as a servant to the world in many ways, including feeding the starving and bringing comfort to the sick. In the Middle Ages in Britain, the monasteries acted as refuges for those in need of food and healing.

If the Church is to be following the example of Jesus, it needs to be unleashed to be a servant to the world.

Way in

Q: In what ways is the Church acting as a servant to the world today?

Introduction to Family

When we look at the life and ministry of Jesus, we see not only somebody who preached and taught, but also one who turned the convention of the society upside down and served those he led.

In the Middle East, honour and ritual cleanliness were very important aspects to Jews. The one showed that they were respected and valued within the community and therefore good followers of Yahweh, and the other enabled them to come before the Holy God and worship him.

My thoughts and notes...

So a Jewish teacher or rabbi was expected to ensure that he was kept holy and ritually clean. There were many things that could affect your situation – who you spent time with, what you touched, how you washed and what you ate, to mention a few.

However, Jesus acted in completely the opposite way to what would have been expected of a holy man. He touched and healed lepers, he spent time with tax collectors and sinners and he washed his disciples' feet, which was a job only a slave would have done.

The creator of the universe was willing to serve the people he created.

Wider Body

The early Church at the beginning of Acts was doing what it had seen Jesus do. Instead of keeping itself away from the poor, the sick and the ritually unclean, it was already reaching out to those who were on the edge and in need.

Bible focus

Read Acts 6:1–7

[1] In those days when the number of disciples was increasing, the Hellenistic Jews among them complained against the Hebraic Jews because their widows were being overlooked in the daily distribution of food. [2] So the Twelve gathered all the disciples together and said, 'It would not be right for us to neglect the ministry of the word of God in order to wait on tables. [3] Brothers and sisters, choose seven men from among you who are known to be full of the Spirit and wisdom. We will turn this responsibility over to them [4] and will give our attention to prayer and the ministry of the word.'

[5] This proposal pleased the whole group. They chose Stephen, a man full of faith and of the Holy Spirit; also Philip, Procorus, Nicanor, Timon, Parmenas, and Nicolas from Antioch, a convert to Judaism. [6] They presented these men to the apostles, who prayed and laid their hands on them.

[7] So the word of God spread. The number of disciples in Jerusalem increased rapidly, and a large number of priests became obedient to the faith.

Q: What strikes you about this passage?

Q: What questions do you have?

Q: How is the early Church serving its community?

his was a time when there was no social care, d women particularly could not hold property. when a woman's husband died, his land and property would be transferred to his next of kin. If she was fortunate to have a son who was old enough to oversee it, then she would be looked after. However, if her children were all girls, then his land would be transferred to a male relative. The widow could then be left with no form of income or way of making a living. We get an insight into this in the book of Ruth, where Naomi returns to her own people in the hope that there will be somebody there who will look after her.

Acts tells us that the early Church was caring for widows and orphans. They were sharing what they had in a common purse, not only with those that had something to put in, but also with those who had nothing to give.

Read Matt 5:1–12

[1] Now when Jesus saw the crowds, he went up on a mountainside and sat down. His disciples came to him, [2] and he began to teach them.

He said:

[3] "Blessed are the poor in spirit,
  for theirs is the kingdom of heaven.
[4] Blessed are those who mourn,
  for they will be comforted.
[5] Blessed are the meek,
  for they will inherit the earth.
[6] Blessed are those who hunger and thirst for righteousness,
  for they will be filled.
[7] Blessed are the merciful,
  for they will be shown mercy.
[8] Blessed are the pure in heart,
  for they will see God.
[9] Blessed are the peacemakers,
  for they will be called children of God.
[10] Blessed are those who are persecuted because of righteousness,
  for theirs is the kingdom of heaven.

[11] "Blessed are you when people insult you, persecute you and falsely say all kinds of evil against you because of me. 12 Rejoice and be glad, because great is your reward in heaven, for in the same way they persecuted the prophets who were before you.

This is another example of Jesus' upside down kingdom.

  Q: Which do you find the hardest to understand?

  Q: Which do you find the hardest to be?

  Q: Create a few of the 'Devil's Beatitudes'.

> My thoughts and notes...

The Church Unleashed as Servant

For example:

Blessed are the rich because they will get richer.

Blessed are the trouble makers – they shall be called my children.

Serving the world and demonstrating God's love through loving others is an important aspect of the servant model. But this is done within a balance of the other models, not at the exclusion of them.

Q: What would the problems with only the servant model?

Q: If the widows and orphans of the early Church were those that had no rights, no protection and no way of ensuring a future, who may the equivalent be today?

Within the Apology of Aristides, an address written to the Emperor Hadrian in AD 137, the author comments on the behaviour of Christians:

Oh emperor, it is the Christians that have sought and found the truth, for they acknowledge God. They do not keep for themselves the goods entrusted to them. They do not covet what belongs to others, but they show love to their neighbours. They do not do to another what they would not like done to themselves. They speak gently to those who oppress them, and in this way, they make their enemies their friends. It has become their passion to do good to their enemies. They live in the awareness of their own smallness. Everyone of them who has anything gives ungrudgingly to the one who has nothing. And if any of them sees a homeless stranger, they bring them into their own home, under their roof. If anyone of them becomes poor while the Christians have nothing to spare, then they fast two or three days until everyone can eat. In this way, they supply for the poor exactly what they need. This, oh emperor, is the rule of life for the Christians. This is how they live.[3]

Q: This was how the early church was described in AD137. How does the church today show signs of acting in similar ways?

Q: In what ways does your church serve the community or neighbourhood it relates to?

Quoted in Cris Rogers, Practicing Resurrection (Authentic Media: Iton Keynes, 2015)

Q: What are the needs in your local neighbourhood and how could your church serve them?

Bible focus

If we are to follow Jesus in how we are to act and behave, then we need to take his servant leadership seriously.

Read John 5:16–22

16 So, because Jesus was doing these things on the Sabbath, the Jewish leaders began to persecute him. 17 In his defense Jesus said to them, "My Father is always at his work to this very day, and I too am working." 18 For this reason they tried all the more to kill him; not only was he breaking the Sabbath, but he was even calling God his own Father, making himself equal with God.

19 Jesus gave them this answer: "Very truly I tell you, the Son can do nothing by himself; he can do only what he sees his Father doing, because whatever the Father does the Son also does. 20 For the Father loves the Son and shows him all he does. Yes, and he will show him even greater works than these, so that you will be amazed. 21 For just as the Father raises the dead and gives them life, even so the Son gives life to whom he is pleased to give it. 22 Moreover, the Father judges no one, but has entrusted all judgment to the Son.

Read 1 John 3:16–18

16 This is how we know what love is: Jesus Christ laid down his life for us. And we ought to lay down our lives for our brothers and sisters. 17 If anyone has material possessions and sees a brother or sister in need but has no pity on them, how can the love of God be in that person? 18 Dear children, let us not love with words or speech but with actions and in truth.

Q: Why does Jesus wash the disciples' feet?

Q: How does this imitate what Jesus sees the Father do?

Jesus does what he sees the Father do, and we in turn are expected to do what we see Jesus doing. As he serves his disciples, even those that will go on to betray him, we are called to serve those around us too. In 1 John we are reminded to love one another and to show our love not only by our words but also by our actions.

Loving and serving others is not always a simple or easy thing to do.

Showing love to those that abuse us.

Showing love to those who take advantage of us.

Showing love to those in addiction.

Sometimes showing love and serving others is to know when to stop giving and to create boundaries. Jesus showed a deep level of compassion and love, but also placed boundaries on his actions and did not always fulfil people's expectations in the way that they wanted.

Q: In what ways do we find it easy to show God's love to one another?

Q: Who do we find it easy to serve and show love to?

Q: Who might we find it hard to serve and show love to?

Response

Take a bowl of water and place in it some sweet-smelling soap product.

Get a hand towel.

Then take it in turns to wash one another's hands saying:

'I wash your hand as a sign of my willingness to love the world and be a sign of Jesus' love to the world.'

You could get some stones from the garden that are covered in mud and dirt and invite the group to wash one each, while imagining that the stone is somebody that they find it hard to serve and love.

Q: How does it feel to be served?

Q: How does it feel to serve?

Prayer

Pray silently for those that you find it hard to love and serve, and invite God to show you ways of engaging with them.

As a group pray for some of the areas where the church serves the world, and in particular, activities in your neighbourhood.

You may wish to come up with a practical activity you could do as a group to serve your neighbourhood and arrange to do it one Saturday or in evening.

The Church Unleashed in Power

▶ Introduction

A key characteristic of both Jesus' ministry and the early Church was the occurrence of miraculous events and signs, things that were not possible that happened supernaturally. These are special ways that God exercises his creative power to bear witness to himself.

In the Bible this has a twofold effect. First, the miracles point to Jesus' divinity in that he has power over the natural order of things. And second, these signs also demonstrate heaven meeting earth as the Kingdom of God comes in Jesus and the power of the Spirit.

At Pentecost there was an outpouring of the Holy Spirit on all the apostles and disciples, which has continued through the years and is still evident today – the gift of the Spirit is promised to all who believe (Acts 2:38-39).

▶ Way in

Q: What are the most fantastic miracles that you have seen? (The majority of miracles in the Gospels and book of Acts are healings, exorcisms, resurrections, control over nature and forgiveness of sins.)

If the group is struggling, here is just one of many stories that we could tell.

When my husband Cris was at college, he was playing squash very enthusiastically and ran into a wall. After suffering with pain for 14 days or so, he was persuaded to go to A&E. When he got there, he had an X-ray and was told that he had broken his collarbone. He then was told that he needed to come back to the fracture clinic the following week. The pain was bad, and there was a lump on his collarbone which he referred to as an egg.

That Sunday evening he attended a church service, where a number of people had that afternoon been trained to pray for healing.

From the front the leader said that somebody thought that God wanted to heal someone with an egg on their shoulder. At that point Cris got up and went to the front to be prayed for. Two teenage lads came forward, who had only that afternoon been taught how to pray for people. They prayed for Cris, and the area of the break felt warm and the pain stopped.

The shoulder felt much better, and Cris felt blessed that God had taken the pain away – but not much more. Until he went to the fracture clinic, where they decided to do another X-ray. When the consultant came in, he was annoyed and cross that they had X-rayed the wrong shoulder. On investigation, they realized that the correct shoulder had been X-rayed, but that it was no longer broken and had been healed!

Q: What are your reactions to miracles, especially healing?

Introduction to power

In our Western society we like things that we can understand. Science and rational thinking, which has natural explanations for things, shape us, and our society is often suspicious of things that seem to have less practical and physical causes.

In the Gospels and Acts, we see plenty of cases where Jesus or the disciples show the power of God by healing people in a variety of ways, including bringing sight to the blind and healing those with leprosy.

These miraculous signs are more than just healings; they are about restoring life to people who had no future; they are about demonstrating the power of God over the natural order; they are about giving a sight of what will happen when Jesus' kingdom rule comes to earth.

Wider Body

The disciples at the beginning of Acts carried on with doing what they had seen Jesus doing. They continue to meet with one another and eat together, they carried on praying and worshipping at the temple and they preached about the kingdom of God.

Bible focus

Read Acts 3:1–16

[1]One day Peter and John were going up to the temple at the time of prayer—at three in the afternoon. [2] Now a man who was lame from birth was being carried to the temple gate called Beautiful, where he was put every day to beg from those going into the temple courts. [3] When he saw Peter and John about to enter, he asked them for money. [4] Peter looked straight at him, as did John. Then Peter said, "Look at us!" [5] So the man gave them his attention, expecting to get something from them.

[6] Then Peter said, "Silver or gold I do not have, but what I do have I give you. In the name of Jesus Christ of Nazareth, walk." [7] Taking him by the right hand, he helped him up, and instantly the man's feet and ankles became strong. [8] He jumped to his feet and began to walk. Then he went with them into the temple courts, walking and jumping, and praising God. [9] When all the people saw him walking and praising God, [10] they recognized him as the same man who used to sit begging at the temple gate called Beautiful, and they were filled with wonder and amazement at what had happened to him.

[11] While the man held on to Peter and John, all the people were astonished and came running to them in the place called Solomon's Colonnade. [12] When Peter saw this, he said to them: "Fellow Israelites, why does this surprise you? Why do you stare at us as if by our own power or godliness we had made this man walk? [13] The God of Abraham, Isaac and Jacob, the God of our fathers, has glorified his servant Jesus. You handed him over to be killed, and you disowned him before Pilate, though he had decided to let him go. [14] You disowned the Holy and Righteous One and asked that a murderer be released to you. [15] You killed the author of life, but God raised him from the dead. We are witnesses of this. By faith in the name of Jesus, this man whom you see and know was made strong. It is Jesus' name and the faith that comes through him that has completely healed him, as you can all see.

Q: What strikes you about this passage?

Q: What questions do you have?

As Peter and John were attending their regular daily prayer time at the temple, they came across a lame beggar. In the Middle East during the time of the early Church, there was no support for those who were unable to work, so if they had no family to support them, they begged for money and food. The Jewish faith had a tradition of supporting those who were less fortunate and giving with dignity to those in need.

The man asked for money, but Peter and John offered him more than that – they restored him to health and therefore gave him a future.

The miracle is a sign of heaven breaking through and changing life on earth. It could be seen as a resurrection moment and a sign of what is to come.

The Church needs to be unleashed to be a place where God's Spirit of power can work through the people to impact the world in heaven-meets-earth moments.

Different churches demonstrate the supernatural power of God through signs and wonders in a variety of ways. Some may go out onto the streets and pray for people, others may have healing and prayer within church at the end of a service, some have regularly advertised services of healing with anointing of oil. You might not feel comfortable with all of these, but if the Church is following the example set by the early Church, it needs to take the power of God seriously and look at how it engages with the supernatural nature of the Holy Spirit.

Q: What do you think was significant about Peter announcing healing in the name of 'Jesus Christ of Nazareth' (v6)? In whose authority was Peter working?

Q: What ways have you seen or heard of the Church demonstrating the supernatural power of God through signs and wonders?

We refer to the supernatural nature of the Church as signs and wonders. The signs are pointers to a future age where 'the time comes for God to restore everything' (v21) and there will be no suffering, and they are signs because they are rare – they are not commonplace or regular. They are also things that cause us and others to wonder as we see things that are wonderful and amazing and, again, rare. Signs and wonders are by definition not common, but that doesn't mean that we can't expect them to happen!

Q: How natural and normal are signs and wonders in your church?

Q: Healing is a commonly talked about supernatural work of God, but is not the only one. What other signs and wonders of God may there be?

Q: What do you think causes us to not see these signs and wonders?

Q: What would activate you to being a part of praying for miracles?

Within the parts of the Body

It can often feel as though the global Church has more stories of miracles than the UK Church. I personally have heard stories of Christian Iranian prisoners praying and walking out of their cells not being seen by their captors; stories of Syrian Christians not being seen by their persecutors who were coming to kill them and North Koreans in secret prayer meetings being visited by Jesus. These are all amazing stories told by Christians around the world. If we are not careful, we can foster the mindset that those things happen elsewhere but would never happen here.

But each of those church communities is made up of individuals who were involved in these signs and wonders.

In the same way, each church in the UK is made up of prayerful followers of Jesus – people like you!

You are a part of a supernatural church of Jesus Christ of Nazareth, and like Peter and John, you personally are invited to administer the work of the Holy Spirit.

Q: Do you feel able to pray for miracles?

Q: It is evident that the early Christians prayed earnestly for signs and wonders (see Acts 4:29–30). How earnestly do you pray for the opportunities to see miracles?

Q: Knowing that there are those around the world seeing amazing miracles every day, does this inspire you to pray for them in the UK?

Some people question whether these miracles were only for the apostles and disciples and not the Church today. Martyn Lloyd-Jones in *The Sovereign Spirit* helpfully reminds us:

It is perfectly clear that in New Testament times, the gospel was authenticated in this way by signs, wonders and miracles of various characters and descriptions . . . Was it only meant to be true of the early church? . . . The Scriptures never anywhere say that these things were only temporary—never! There is no such statement anywhere.[4]

---

4   Martyn Lloyd-Jones, The Sovereign Spirit, (Harold Shaw: Wheaton, 1986) pp. 31-32

Q: Have you ever wondered this same question?

Q: How would you argue that miracles are for today and not just the early Church?

God doesn't always give us the miracles we ask for. If a miracle doesn't happen, we shouldn't blame ourselves or feel that our faith is inadequate. This world is still affected and influenced by the fall and is not perfect. Even though Jesus has come and proclaimed victory over sin, we are still in a period of waiting for a full realisation of God's rule to be re-established. That will happen when Jesus returns at the end of time. We are stuck in a period of the 'now and the not-yet': We will see signs of the future but there are still times when we are fully aware of the fallen nature of the world. In the meantime, we keep trusting God that he will work all things for good in the end. But we also shouldn't be discouraged from asking God to work supernaturally in future.

Q: How can we make sure we keep trusting God if a miracle doesn't happen?

Miracles can make evangelism much easier. There are at least 17 times where miracles which happened in the book of Acts helped lead to conversions. The clearest examples are in Acts 9:34–35 and 9:40, 42. Peter heals Aeneas, and Luke says, 'And all the residents of Lydda and Sharon saw him, and they turned to the Lord.' Peter raises Tabitha from the dead, and Luke says, 'It became known to all Joppa, and many believed in the Lord.'

Q: Do you know anyone who has come to faith from a miracle? Can you share the story?

Tip:

Do not wait to get into a healing course before you start praying for miracles. Courses can be helpful, but you already have what you need. Praying in the name of Jesus, with the authority he has already given you is everything you need. When you accepted Jesus as Lord, he had already equipped you with his authority to do his work. Remember you don't do miracles; Jesus does miracles. We are nothing more than the conduit of his presence. Also remember that signs and wonders may be strange to us but they are not strange to God. Miracles are just what God does and what seems supernatural to us is just natural to God. So have confidence not in yourself but in Jesus.

Response

Pray – Pray for more opportunities to pray for miracles.

Ask – How might you create opportunities within your life or church for more signs and wonders?

Practise – Why not pray for those in the room needing a miracle? This could be a great training opportunity or testimony moment.

Prayer

Heavenly Father,

We rejoice in the signs of your kingdom found in the Gospels, through the stories of the Church, both old and new. Fill us with the healing power of your Spirit. Cast out anything that would stop us from confidently praying for signs of your Kingdom. Mend in us what is broken, restore in us the call of the early Church. Would we play our part in partnering with you in your Kingdom work.

Would your church be known again as a place of signs and wonders of your power.

Would we be known as people who administer your presence.

In the name of Jesus Christ of Nazareth,

Amen.

The Church Unleashed as Herald

 ## Introduction

A key aspect of the Church that was very prevalent in Acts is proclamation and preaching of the good news of Jesus' life, death and resurrection. The apostles and disciples spent a great deal of their time and energy talking to people, groups and crowds about Jesus' life, death and resurrection.

In this model the Church acts as a *herald*. We use the word in Christmas carols to describe the angels in the nativity who went to tell the shepherds of Jesus' birth and then invited them to come and worship the Baby. If the Church is to be effective in the world, it needs to be unleashed to be a herald proclaiming Jesus and inviting others to come and worship him.

 ## Way in

This model brings us to evangelism, and many of us will have our own feelings and thoughts about this subject.

Q: How do you feel when you hear the word evangelism and what images does it conjure up?

The word and subject may make some think of a person standing and shouting at people in the street or large arenas filled with people and an appeal to 'go forward' if you believe. Others may have experience with more personal or relational forms of evangelism.

This is an opportunity for people to air their fears or excitement at the word. Ensure that people's feelings and experiences are held and acknowledged.

Q: When did you last have some amazing good news to share? This might be an engagement, a new job, a baby, or a win in a competition, for example.

Q: How did you feel when you heard the news?

Q: How did you feel when sharing it with other people?

For the early Church, the news that Jesus had been resurrected from the dead and then ascended into heaven was the best news that we have ever had – it's no wonder that they wanted to tell everyone about it!

My thoughts and notes...

Introduction to herald

There was a strong emphasis on telling people about Jesus in the early Church. This was, as we've said above, influenced by the amazing experience that the disciples had, but it was also affected by the belief that Jesus would return within the apostles' lifespans. Therefore, the early Church thought it was of paramount importance that the people were told about the Messiah; if they weren't, then they would not be with Jesus when he returned.

We find many examples within the book of Acts of the disciples and the apostles telling first the Jews and then the Gentiles about Jesus' death and resurrection. The early Church was a loud and strong herald to the people of the world.

 # Within the wider Body

Most churches preach and proclaim Jesus' life, death and resurrection to those within the community and on the edges and outside of the neighbourhood. These can be in organized ways or more individual personal ones.

Q: Think about your church now – when and how does it preach the good news of Jesus?

Bible focus

Read Acts 2:14–41

14 Then Peter stood up with the Eleven, raised his voice and addressed the crowd: 'Fellow Jews and all of you who live in Jerusalem, let me explain this to you; listen carefully to what I say. 15 These people are not drunk, as you suppose. It's only nine in the morning! 16 No, this is what was spoken by the prophet Joel:

17 "In the last days, God says,
    I will pour out my Spirit on all people.
Your sons and daughters will prophesy,
    your young men will see visions,
    your old men will dream dreams.

18 Even on my servants, both men and women,
    I will pour out my Spirit in those days,
    and they will prophesy.
19 I will show wonders in the heavens above
    and signs on the earth below,
    blood and fire and billows of smoke.
20 The sun will be turned to darkness

and the moon to blood
before the coming of the great and glorious day of the Lord.
[21] And everyone who calls
on the name of the Lord will be saved."

[22] Fellow Israelites, listen to this: Jesus of Nazareth was a man accredited by God to you by miracles, wonders and signs, which God did among you through him, as you yourselves know. [23] This man was handed over to you by God's deliberate plan and foreknowledge; and you, with the help of wicked men, put him to death by nailing him to the cross. [24] But God raised him from the dead, freeing him from the agony of death, because it was impossible for death to keep its hold on him. [25] David said about him:

"I saw the Lord always before me.
Because he is at my right hand,
I will not be shaken.
[26] Therefore my heart is glad and my tongue rejoices;
my body also will rest in hope,
[27] because you will not abandon me to the realm of the dead,
you will not let your holy one see decay.
[28] You have made known to me the paths of life;
you will fill me with joy in your presence."

[29] Fellow Israelites, I can tell you confidently that the patriarch David died and was buried, and his tomb is here to this day. [30] But he was a prophet and knew that God had promised him on oath that he would place one of his descendants on his throne. [31] Seeing what was to come, he spoke of the resurrection of the Messiah, that he was not abandoned to the realm of the dead, nor did his body see decay. [32] God has raised this Jesus to life, and we are all witnesses of it. [33] Exalted to the right hand of God, he has received from the Father the promised Holy Spirit and has poured out what you now see and hear. [34] For David did not ascend to heaven, and yet he said,

"The Lord said to my Lord:
'Sit at my right hand
[35] until I make your enemies
a footstool for your feet.'"

[36] Therefore let all Israel be assured of this: God has made this Jesus, whom you crucified, both Lord and Messiah.'

[37] When the people heard this, they were cut to the heart and said to Peter and the other apostles, 'Brothers, what shall we do?'

[38] Peter replied, 'Repent and be baptised, every one of you, in the name of Jesus Christ for the forgiveness of your sins. And you will receive the gift of the Holy Spirit. [39] The promise is for you and your children and for all who are far off – for all whom the Lord our God will call.'

[40] With many other words he warned them; and he pleaded with them, 'Save yourselves from this corrupt generation.' [41] Those who accepted his message were baptised, and about three thousand were added to their number that day.

Q: What strikes you about this passage?

Q: What questions do you have?

This passage is set immediately after Pentecost – the disciples had just received the Holy Spirit upon them individually while they were together in the upper room.

There were crowds of people within Jerusalem who were there to celebrate the Jewish festival of first fruits. This was when the Jews brought an offering of their first crops to the temple as an offering of worship in thanks to God, a bit like a harvest festival. Peter, the fisherman more known up to that point for putting his foot in it, stood up and spoke to them about Jesus. This was the man who previously denied Jesus, but here, after the outpouring of the spirit, preached the first of the Church's evangelistic sermons and saw many become Christians.

It has been said that the 'Church is essentially a kerygmatic community which holds aloft, through the preached Word, the wonderful deeds of God in past history, particularly his mighty act in Jesus Christ.' [5]

The word *kerygmatic* describes the act of preaching that calls for the hearer to have faith in Jesus.

Q: Do you think this is true – is the Church a community that preaches God's deeds?

Q: In what way does the wider Church today preach God's deeds?

In this model the Church is not merely a body that preaches the word but is actually a herald that continually preaches the truth of Jesus' life, death and resurrection to those within it and those outside of it.

---

5   *Richard McBrien, Church, The Continuing Quest (Newman, New York, 1970) p. 11, quoted in Dulles, p. 70*

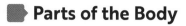

Parts of the Body

Read Acts 17:15–31

¹⁵ Those who escorted Paul brought him to Athens and then left with instructions for Silas and Timothy to join him as soon as possible.

¹⁶ While Paul was waiting for them in Athens, he was greatly distressed to see that the city was full of idols. ¹⁷ So he reasoned in the synagogue with both Jews and God-fearing Greeks, as well as in the marketplace day by day with those who happened to be there. ¹⁸ A group of Epicurean and Stoic philosophers began to debate with him. Some of them asked, "What is this babbler trying to say?" Others remarked, "He seems to be advocating foreign gods." They said this because Paul was preaching the good news about Jesus and the resurrection. ¹⁹ Then they took him and brought him to a meeting of the Areopagus, where they said to him, "May we know what this new teaching is that you are presenting? ²⁰ You are bringing some strange ideas to our ears, and we would like to know what they mean." ²¹ (All the Athenians and the foreigners who lived there spent their time doing nothing but talking about and listening to the latest ideas.)

²² Paul then stood up in the meeting of the Areopagus and said: "People of Athens! I see that in every way you are very religious. ²³ For as I walked around and looked carefully at your objects of worship, I even found an altar with this inscription: to an unknown god. So you are ignorant of the very thing you worship—and this is what I am going to proclaim to you.

²⁴ "The God who made the world and everything in it is the Lord of heaven and earth and does not live in temples built by human hands. ²⁵ And he is not served by human hands, as if he needed anything. Rather, he himself gives everyone life and breath and everything else. ²⁶ From one man he made all the nations, that they should inhabit the whole earth; and he marked out their appointed times in history and the boundaries of their lands. ²⁷ God did this so that they would seek him and perhaps reach out for him and find him, though he is not far from any one of us. ²⁸ 'For in him we live and move and have our being.' As some of your own poets have said, 'We are his offspring.'

²⁹ "Therefore since we are God's offspring, we should not think that the divine being is like gold or silver or stone—an image made by human design and skill. ³⁰ In the past God overlooked such ignorance, but now he commands all people everywhere to repent. ³¹ For he has set a day when he will judge the world with justice by the man he has appointed. He has given proof of this to everyone by raising him from the dead."

Q: What strikes you about this passage?

Q: What questions do you have?

Q: What does Paul do in Athens before preaching?

Q: Why do you think he uses the image of the unknown God?

In the passage above, Paul had arrived in Athens. As he usually did, he began preaching about Jesus. However, when we look at the sermon he gave, it is obvious that he had spent time going around the city and getting to know it and the people. He saw the multitude of gods, and even the unknown one that the Athenians had to cover themselves. He then took what he knew about the people and the culture and used that as a way to articulate the gospel to those around him.

Read Matt 28:16–20

[16] Then the eleven disciples went to Galilee, to the mountain where Jesus had told them to go. [17] When they saw him, they worshiped him; but some doubted. [18] Then Jesus came to them and said, "All authority in heaven and on earth has been given to me. [19] Therefore go and make disciples of all nations, baptizing them in the name of the Father and of the Son and of the Holy Spirit, [20] and teaching them to obey everything I have commanded you. And surely I am with you always, to the very end of the age."

Q: What strikes you about this passage?

Q: What questions do you have?

Q: How do we make disciples of all nations?

Some scholars argue that the instruction 'go and make' is more accurately translated as 'in your going make.' This is due to the tense used in the original Greek, which doesn't have an easy translation in English.

Q: What difference would it make if we interpret the passage as 'in your going make' rather than 'go and make'?

Jesus' last instruction to us was pretty clear – we were to go to those around us, near and far, and tell them about his life, death and resurrection.

Q: Where has your daily life taken you this week and how have you managed to talk about Jesus' good news?

Q: Where may your daily life take you next week, and how could you share Jesus with those you encounter?

▶ Response

We have looked at how the Church unleashed needs to be a herald proclaiming and preaching the good news of Jesus' life, death and resurrection. For some of us, that isn't a problem;

we find it easy to talk about him and see people come to faith. For many of us, however, this is hard and we often worry about how we are to do it, what do we say and what will happen.

So as the response, we are introducing a method of sharing faith that is simple and accessible to most people. It is very similar to the way that Paul shared his faith in Acts 17.

It's called 'their story, your story, God's story'.[6]

Their story

First, he had taken the opportunity to find out the story of the people he was talking to. Unlike when he got caught out in Lystra where they thought he was a Greek god, he had walked about Athens and got to know the community a bit. So he began by talking about their story.

We start by listening, focusing on the person that we are engaging with – what is their experience of God, of the Church and faith, what is their life like, what are they going through. We begin where they are at the moment. Not judging or sensing, but listening, just as Jesus did with the Samaritan woman.

My story

Then you find overlaps between their story and your story. You share things that connect to the person and where God has impacted you. This is the opportunity to give your testimony, to tell the story of your journey and engagement with God. You don't need to tell them everything, only the things that are connected with them and that feel relevant to the story that they have told you.

Q: Can you tell your testimony in 2 minutes (around 30 words)?

Q: Practice writing it and speaking it to one another.

Q: See if you can come up with three versions of your testimony, all of which have a different focus.

My thoughts and notes...

For more on this, see Phil Knox, Story Bearer: How to share your faith with your friends (IVP: London, 2020)

God's story – the big story

From that, you then explain, like Paul did, the big story – the one that points to Jesus' life, death and resurrection. Again, you don't start at Genesis and tell them everything through to Revelation and beyond. Instead, you give the highlights that connect with what God has done for you and the story the person has told you.

Prayer

Spend a few minutes asking God to show you three people that he would like you to share His story with. Then spend a few minutes praying for opportunities to listen to their stories and for wisdom to know what parts of your story link them to God's story.

You may like to share with the group the names of those you are praying for so that everyone can hold them in prayer. Although for confidentiality reasons, you may like to assign them a letter or number – God knows who we are praying for even if we don't.

Heavenly Father, we thank you that Jesus came and lived amongst us, hearing the stories of those he met. We thank you that he shared his story with us on the cross, enabling us to understand and engage in your story. Help us this week to do the same, that others may also be amazed and inspired by Your Story.

Amen

The Church Unleashed as Organization

▶ Introduction

The word organization or institution can generate different emotions for different people; some of us shudder and shrivel inside as we connect church structure and institution with something that stops and strangles the presence of God. But this doesn't have to be the case.

Imagine an outdoor water tap. If you tried to water the garden from it directly, you'd turn it on but it would only gush straight down to the floor. However, if you attach a hosepipe, then suddenly you can direct all that water over the whole garden, just where it is needed! The Church unleashed as organization and institution isn't about confining and limiting the dynamic nature of God but about creating flows and systems that allow the Spirit to do his work.

This section is going to look at how the Church unleashed as organization can enable it to work more effectively in the world.

▶ Way in

We all have our own peculiarities that we often only realize when others comment on them. We all have our own traditions, ways of doing things and methods of organizing, perhaps ways of celebrating milestones or festivals.

Our family always goes out for breakfast the first day of the summer holidays, to celebrate the end of another school year and to connect together. We also have a different 'Happy Birthday' song we sing, which has come down from my grandparents.

What celebration traditions do you have? You might like to think of how you celebrate Christmas or birthdays.

In the same way we often have habits that help us to live life more effectively and efficiently.

What are your regular habits? You may think of things like:

- What time you brush your teeth?
- What day do you do the shopping?
- How do you organize your books or DVDs on the shelves?

◗ Introduction to organization

Traditions and habits can help us live life in healthy and effective ways, or they can constrain and limit us. Being organized can help you find something, but somebody who suffers from OCD (Obsessive Compulsive Disorder) can find that their life is limited and constrained by order and organization.

As Christians and the Church, we can develop habits and organization that help things run well and that make the everyday things simpler and easier to do. This can release us to have more time and energy for mission and ministry. However, sometimes these things can take over, and become so important and take up some much of our time that we are restricted in what we are able to do. This session will look at Acts to see where the Church incorporated organization and how that released it, but also how, at times, it needed to be challenged by God to focus on the important things. We will then examine how the same can be true for our own lives as individuals.

◗ Wider body

All churches have structures and traditions to some degree that help facilitate things. These can be as simple as to how to start a service or how to organize who makes the coffee to as detailed as how to appoint a new leader or how the accounts are prepared.

Q: Can you briefly identify a few structures and traditions within your own church that help bring life to the community?

◗ Bible focus

Read Acts 6:1–7

[1]In those days when the number of disciples was increasing, the Hellenistic Jews among them complained against the Hebraic Jews because their widows were being overlooked in the daily distribution of food. [2] So the Twelve gathered all the disciples together and said, 'It would not be right for us to neglect the ministry of the word of God in order to wait on tables. [3] Brothers and sisters, choose seven men from among you who are known to be full of the Spirit and wisdom. We will turn this responsibility over to them [4] and will give our attention to prayer and the ministry of the word.'

[5] This proposal pleased the whole group. They chose Stephen, a man full of faith

and of the Holy Spirit; also Philip, Procorus, Nicanor, Timon, Parmenas, and Nicolas from Antioch, a convert to Judaism. [6] They presented these men to the apostles, who prayed and laid their hands on them.

[7] So the word of God spread. The number of disciples in Jerusalem increased rapidly, and a large number of priests became obedient to the faith.

Q: What strikes you about this passage?

Q: What questions do you have?

The early Church grew quickly in the first few chapters of Acts. But then problems arose over the distribution of food. Since everyone brought what they had and put it together, it was then necessary for it to be allocated. There were arguments about favouritism, which led to complaining to the apostles. So the apostles needed to do something and decided to appoint a number of leaders who were wise and full of the Holy Spirit to oversee the distribution of the food.

They selected the people to help and prayed for them. A structure and a system was put into place to help ensure the food was distributed justly.

Verse 7 shows us what happened next. Just after they had created some structure to help with the organization, the numbers again grew quickly. We could speculate about the reasons for this: Maybe the apostles were no longer dealing with complaints, maybe the Church looked better from the outside because everyone was being treated equally – the reality is, we don't know. But we do know that following the organization, God added to the numbers of those being saved.

Q: How do you think the development of the team helped their work?

Q: What would you have done differently?

However, the opposite is also evident in Acts, where structure and traditions hampered the spread of the gospel so God had to do something to change them:

The birth of the Church was from the Jewish faith. Most of the early followers were Jewish, and they were still following many of the laws and commands found in the Old Testament. This included restricting what was eaten. Leviticus is very clear about what food can and cannot be eaten.

But God's plan was to unleash it onto the world! So needed to reshape some of the traditions and

My thoughts and notes...

structures to enable this. He started this by giving Peter a vision of all the food he was not allowed to eat under Levitical Law:

Read Acts 10:9–23

⁹ About noon the following day as they were on their journey and approaching the city, Peter went up on the roof to pray. ¹⁰ He became hungry and wanted something to eat, and while the meal was being prepared, he fell into a trance. ¹¹ He saw heaven opened and something like a large sheet being let down to earth by its four corners. ¹² It contained all kinds of four-footed animals, as well as reptiles and birds. ¹³ Then a voice told him, "Get up, Peter. Kill and eat."

¹⁴ "Surely not, Lord!" Peter replied. "I have never eaten anything impure or unclean."

¹⁵ The voice spoke to him a second time, "Do not call anything impure that God has made clean."

¹⁶ This happened three times, and immediately the sheet was taken back to heaven.

¹⁷ While Peter was wondering about the meaning of the vision, the men sent by Cornelius found out where Simon's house was and stopped at the gate. ¹⁸ They called out, asking if Simon who was known as Peter was staying there.

¹⁹ While Peter was still thinking about the vision, the Spirit said to him, "Simon, three[a] men are looking for you. ²⁰ So get up and go downstairs. Do not hesitate to go with them, for I have sent them."

²¹ Peter went down and said to the men, "I'm the one you're looking for. Why have you come?"

²² The men replied, "We have come from Cornelius the centurion. He is a righteous and God-fearing man, who is respected by all the Jewish people. A holy angel told him to ask you to come to his house so that he could hear what you have to say." ²³ Then Peter invited the men into the house to be his guests.

At this point in history, Jews were not allowed into a Gentile (non-Jewish) home. But this would seriously limit the work of the Church. So God had to speak directly to Peter to get the early Church to alter some of its structures and beliefs to make it more mission-minded.

Read Acts 10:34–48

³⁴ Then Peter began to speak: "I now realize how true it is that God does not show favoritism ³⁵ but accepts from every nation the one who fears him and does what is right. ³⁶ You know the message God sent to the people of Israel, announcing the good news of peace through Jesus Christ, who is Lord of all. ³⁷ You know what has happened throughout the province of Judea, beginning in Galilee after the baptism that John preached— ³⁸ how God anointed Jesus of Nazareth with the Holy Spirit and power, and how he went around doing good and healing all who were under the power of the devil, because God was with him.

³⁹ "We are witnesses of everything he did in the country of the Jews and in Jerusalem

hey killed him by hanging him on a cross, ⁴⁰ but God raised him from the dead on he third day and caused him to be seen. ⁴¹ He was not seen by all the people, but by witnesses whom God had already chosen—by us who ate and drank with him after e rose from the dead. ⁴² He commanded us to preach to the people and to testify hat he is the one whom God appointed as judge of the living and the dead. ⁴³ All the rophets testify about him that everyone who believes in him receives forgiveness of ns through his name."

While Peter was still speaking these words, the Holy Spirit came on all who heard he message. ⁴⁵ The circumcised believers who had come with Peter were astonished hat the gift of the Holy Spirit had been poured out even on Gentiles. ⁴⁶ For they eard them speaking in tongues[a] and praising God.

hen Peter said, ⁴⁷ "Surely no one can stand in the way of their being baptized with vater. They have received the Holy Spirit just as we have." ⁴⁸ So he ordered that they e baptized in the name of Jesus Christ. Then they asked Peter to stay with them for few days.

ter learnt the lesson that God was teaching and anged his views. Again at the end of the passage, ople were baptised – and the Church grew, this he through being challenged by God to change its uctures.

Response

Q: What structures and traditions might your church have that helps those within it to focus on mission and ministry? Thank God for them.

Q: Prayerfully ask God to help you see those things that may make mission and ministry hard and ask him to give wisdom to know how to go forward.

Q: A bishop said: 'I have never seen a church organization grow because of its structures, but have seen a church organization fail to grow because of its poor structures.' How do you think organization connects with the work of the Spirit?

Parts of the Body

e all have traditions and habits to help us in r faith walk: praying in the morning, receiving mmunion, meeting with others.

Q: What habits do you have that help with your aith in your daily life?

ad Acts 3:1

ne day Peter and John were going up to the temple at the time of prayer—at three the afternoon.

Peter and John were heading to the temple at 3pm to pray. This was one of the regular times of prayer that the Jewish people had. This was still at the beginning of the birth of the Church so the disciples were carrying on doing much of what they did as Jews – regularly praying. We also have a number of examples in the gospel of Jesus withdrawing to pray.

This regular prayer routine was one that in this incidence allowed Peter to pray for the beggar's healing and to again see others come to know more about the freedom that Jesus offers.

Regular prayer times and routines can help us remain in relationship with God, connected to him, being fed by him and not just reliant on our own whims or strength.

However, there are also times that Jesus challenged the 'religious' nature of the Pharisees, and of course Peter later realized that some of the traditions, for example, not going into a Gentile's house, restricted the spread of the gospel.

Are there times that our structures or rhythms may be hampering our ability to be unleashed on the world, or may there be some that would help us engage with Jesus more deeply and be fuelled to serve him better?

Ideas for silent prayerful reflection

Q: What organization or rhythm would help you follow Jesus more deeply?

Q: What habits or rhythms may God be challenging you to look at again as they may be getting in the way of witnessing in his world?

Response and prayer

3-2-1 simple discipline (making disciples)

On the following page is a resource from *www.makingdisciples.com*. It is a suggestion of a simple discipline that encourages us daily to read scripture, pray and listen to God.

Encourage one another to try doing it this week as a way of focusing on God more.

6min. Retreat

Each day we need to stop and remind ourselves what's important. We can get so focused on the now that we forget to focus on the eternal. A 6 minute retreat each day helps us build the relationship with God that will sustain us today and tomorrow.

Bible   3 min.

Take out the Bible - either paper or digital. You can choose to read through one book or gospel - we would say go short, bit by bit and allow yourself to take it in. You could use a study guide to give you passages to read.

Take a small chunk, read it and ask yourself 3 questions:

1. What does this tell me about me?

2. What does this tell me about God?

3. What do I need to do to take the passage and live it?

Pray   2 min.

God loves your voice. He loves to hear what you have to say. He loves to hear you cry, laugh and complain. Your prayers don't need to be clever, simply say either in your mind or our loud what's going on for you. Share thanksgiving as well as your needs. Simply start by saying something like "Hello God", "Dear Father" or "God come find me". Then just go for it.

Listen   1 min.

God wants to talk as well as listen, so take a moment to listen to him. Sometimes you might get a sense of what he is saying. Some people talk about a feeling. You might just feel his presence. All of this is good stuff. If you hear nothing, don't get stressed. You still it with him.

End by saying "Amen" (it just means 'so be it').

The Church Unleashed as Sign

Introduction

Another way of seeing the Church is as a *sign to the world* – a sign that does more than just point the way, but is an example, an illustration, a visible emblem of Christ's presence in the world. Some traditions of the Church refer to this as a *sacrament*, but in order to avoid the confusion between that and other uses of the word sacrament, we are using the word *sign*.

The Church can be an illustration and a sign of the love and grace of God in the world. This is more than the Church just talking about it; it is a way of people who don't know what God is like to see it within the work and life of the Church. To see where the Church shows holiness, love, grace and forgiveness, and through that to see what it means for God to show all those things to the world.

Way in

The Church is depicted in many forms of media: films, books and TV, for example. For people with little or no church involvement, these can be the only versions of the Church they come across. Some of these are positive and some we may see as negative, but either way they act as a sign of what the Church represents today.

> Q: What examples of the Church have you seen in books, films or TV, and what aspects of the Church have they shown? Examples may range from the use of the church and symbols in programmes to defeat vampires, to the work of the nuns in the show 'Call the Midwife'.

> Q: What aspects of the church do they draw on and point out?

> Q: Have you ever had conversations with people outside the Church as a result of these representations?

Introduction to sign

The early church was a community of people who all believed that Jesus had not only died but had also been resurrected. Originally, they gathered together as friends and extended family where they cared for one another, worshipped together and ate together. But their emphasis was on preaching and telling other people about Jesus' death and resurrection.

When we encounter the early church at the beginning of Acts, Jesus had just ascended into heaven and said that he will return. It is hardly surprising that they understood this as meaning that he would return imminently – certainly within their lifetimes.

So, the urgency was to ensure that as many people as possible believed in Jesus before he came back. The early church then emphasized this and was a sign pointing to Jesus' death and resurrection.

However, when we look at Paul's missionary journeys and his later letters, we begin to see a church that has realized that Jesus is not returning as soon as they thought. They were then concerned with how they lived out the truth of the resurrection in the waiting for Jesus' return. This is the focus of some of Paul's letters to help the Church work out what it meant to be a sign of the kingdom while waiting for its arrival.

Wider body

Q: Think about your own church – what does it point to about who Jesus is?

You might like to think about what people will understand about the Gospel when they visit your church or activities – not just what they hear, but what might they experience.

Bible focus

A significant change in the emphasis of the community and early church happens in Chapter 10 of Acts. Up to that point, the Church had continued to act as Jews who recognized that the Messiah had come – sticking to the restrictions that were set by God's law given to Moses, and the rules and interpretations added by rabbis, which included limitations on what to eat and wear and the practice of circumcision.

Read Acts 10:9–29, 34–35

About noon the following day as they were on their journey and approaching the city, Peter went up on the roof to pray. [10] He became hungry and wanted something to eat, and while the meal was being prepared, he fell into a trance. [11] He saw heaven opened and something like a large sheet being let down to earth by its four corners. [12] It contained all kinds of four-footed animals, as well as reptiles and birds. [13] Then a voice told him, 'Get up, Peter. Kill and eat.'

[14] 'Surely not, Lord!' Peter replied. 'I have never eaten anything impure or unclean.'

[15] The voice spoke to him a second time, 'Do not call anything impure that God has made clean.'

[16] This happened three times, and immediately the sheet was taken back to heaven.

[17] While Peter was wondering about the meaning of the vision, the men sent by Cornelius found out where Simon's house was and stopped at the gate. [18] They called out, asking if Simon who was known as Peter was staying there.

[19] While Peter was still thinking about the vision, the Spirit said to him, 'Simon, three men are looking for you. [20] So get up and go downstairs. Do not hesitate to go with them, for I have sent them.'

[21] Peter went down and said to the men, 'I'm the one you're looking for. Why have you come?'

[22] The men replied, 'We have come from Cornelius the centurion. He is a righteous and God-fearing man, who is respected by all the Jewish people. A holy angel told him to ask you to come to his house so that he could hear what you have to say.' [23] Then Peter invited the men into the house to be his guests.

The next day Peter started out with them, and some of the believers from Joppa went along. [24] The following day he arrived in Caesarea. Cornelius was expecting them and had called together his relatives and close friends. [25] As Peter entered the house, Cornelius met him and fell at his feet in reverence. [26] But Peter made him get up. 'Stand up,' he said, 'I am only a man myself.'

[27] While talking with him, Peter went inside and found a large gathering of people. [28] He said to them: 'You are well aware that it is against our law for a Jew to associate with or visit a Gentile. But God has shown me that I should not call anyone impure or unclean. [29] So when I was sent for, I came without raising any objection. May I ask why you sent for me?'

Peter had a vision from God, which challenged the restrictions on what the Jews could and couldn't eat. This was a radical change for the early church! After the vision Peter realized that the truth of Jesus' death and resurrection was not only for the Jews – but also for the Gentiles. The Gentiles could then be received into the Church, without first having to become Jews. Peter took this message to the wider church community. The Church was opening up its doors and becoming a sign to the world of Jesus' grace for all – not just the Jews.

The Church was becoming a sign of the heavenly kingdom when all would be accepted and there was no Jew or Gentile.

My thoughts and notes...

Q: What difference would it have made to the Church if Peter hadn't had his vision?

Q: Which of you would not have been able to be part of the Church?

However, one of the weaknesses of the Church's focus on being a sign to the world is that the world may not always understand the meaning of the sign.

Read Acts 14:1–18

[1] At Iconium Paul and Barnabas went as usual into the Jewish synagogue. There they spoke so effectively that a great number of Jews and Greeks believed. [2] But the Jews who refused to believe stirred up the other Gentiles and poisoned their minds against the brothers. [3] So Paul and Barnabas spent considerable time there, speaking boldly for the Lord, who confirmed the message of his grace by enabling them to perform signs and wonders. [4] The people of the city were divided; some sided with the Jews, others with the apostles. [5] There was a plot afoot among both Gentiles and Jews, together with their leaders, to mistreat them and stone them. [6] But they found out about it and fled to the Lycaonian cities of Lystra and Derbe and to the surrounding country, [7] where they continued to preach the gospel.

[8] In Lystra there sat a man who was lame. He had been that way from birth and had never walked. [9] He listened to Paul as he was speaking. Paul looked directly at him, saw that he had faith to be healed [10] and called out, "Stand up on your feet!" At that, the man jumped up and began to walk.

+ When the crowd saw what Paul had done, they shouted in the Lycaonian language, "The gods have come down to us in human form!" [12] Barnabas they called Zeus, and Paul they called Hermes because he was the chief speaker. [13] The priest of Zeus, whose temple was just outside the city, brought bulls and wreaths to the city gates because he and the crowd wanted to offer sacrifices to them.

[14] But when the apostles Barnabas and Paul heard of this, they tore their clothes and rushed out into the crowd, shouting: [15] "Friends, why are you doing this? We too are only human, like you. We are bringing you good news, telling you to turn from these worthless things to the living God, who made the heavens and the earth and the sea and everything in them. [16] In the past, he let all nations go their own way. [17] Yet he has not left himself without testimony: He has shown kindness by giving you rain from heaven and crops in their seasons; he provides you with plenty of food and fills your hearts with joy." [18] Even with these words, they had difficulty keeping the crowd from sacrificing to them.

Lystra, Paul and Barnabas healed a lame man in sus' name. The healings demonstrated not only e power of Jesus but were also a visual sign of e Isaiah quote that Luke reports Jesus claiming r himself (Luke 4:18). However, the community Lystra, instead of acknowledging Jesus' power, ed to worship Paul and Barnabas as gods. This was ked to a legend that years before, the gods visited illage and only an elderly couple acknowledged them and gave them hospitality. This resulted in the couple being blessed and the rest of the village being destroyed! So when Lystra saw the miracle that Paul and Barnabas performed, they assumed that the two are Greek gods. Paul and Barnabas then had to explain to the villagers that they were not gods and clarify what the sign was and who Jesus was/is.

The Church being unleashed on the world as a sign allows those who are around it to be pointed to Jesus and the resurrection truth. However, there are times that those on the outside may misunderstand the signs and put their own perspective on it.

Response

Q: In what ways does your church act as a sign of Jesus?

Q: Are there any things that may be misunderstood?

Q: Have you seen other churches doing anything interesting or creative that acts as a sign?

Parts of the Body

Just as the Church acts as a sign to the world, showing what it means to have grace and forgiveness and to preach the good news, for many people, individual Christians are the closest signs of that truth that they experience. For many people, we are the only Bible that they will ever read.

A Roman historian Tertullian, when reflecting on the actions of the Church, said that pagans (non-Christians) may look at the Church and say to one another 'look how these Christians love one another.'

Read 2 Corinthians 3:1–5

[1] Are we beginning to commend ourselves again? Or do we need, like some people, letters of recommendation to you or from you? [2] You yourselves are our letter, written on our hearts, known and read by everyone. [3] You show that you are a letter from Christ, the result of our ministry, written not with ink but with the Spirit of the living God, not on tablets of stone but on tablets of human hearts.

[4] Such confidence we have through Christ before God. [5] Not that we are competent in ourselves to claim anything for ourselves, but our competence comes from God.

Q: What strikes you about this passage?

Q: What questions do you have?

In the past when people travelled, they would often take a letter of recommendation that would let the people they met know who they were and who vouched for them. It would often have a seal on it as proof that it came from the king or rulers. Paul was telling the Corinthians that they were a letter of recommendation from Christ for him; their behaviour, personality and faith pointed to Jesus and his love, grace and forgiveness. For many people around us, we are the only letter of recommendation that they see.

Q: How do you feel about being a letter of recommendation?

Q: What aspects of Jesus does your letter point to?

Q: How could people misinterpret the things you do or why you do them and how could you make it clearer?

Q: Who do you know that inspires you to be a sign?

Response

As a response think about the activities, events and things that your church does that you like, and identify how these work as a sign of Jesus and his kingdom. Put them into the chart on the next page..

Then reverse the process. What aspect of the Good News would you like to point your neighbourhood to and how could you achieve that?

Top 10 things that you love that your church does

How is this a sign of Jesus and his kingdom?

What could you do/organise/plan to achieve this?

What one thing would you like to point your neighbourhood to of Jesus' kingdom?

Prayer

- Pray for all the things that your church represents that point the neighbourhood and wider community to Jesus' kingdom.

- Pray for opportunities to point those we engage with during the day to Jesus' grace forgiveness and love.

The Church Unleashed as Disciple

Introduction

In Jesus' time there were many rabbis who gathered disciples around them to teach them the scriptures and help them to understand what they meant and how they were to live them out. There was a phrase within the Jewish tradition that talked about the disciples being covered in the dust from the shoes of the rabbis they followed. This type of teaching was not only sitting and listening to the rabbis, it was also living alongside them and following them as they lived their lives. As you followed your rabbi closely, you watched him live and react, and from that you saw a great example of what it meant to follow Yahweh. The disciples were said to follow the rabbis so closely that they would be covered in the dust from the teacher's shoes.

The Church is also a community of disciples, a group of people who are committed to journey alongside one another, learning from each other, encouraging and challenging one another. We are called to follow Jesus so closely, learning from all that he has shown us in his life, death and resurrection that we would be 'covered in the dust from his shoes'.

The Church needs to be unleashed to be a disciple if it is to effectively minister to the world around it.

Way in

It is well known that people who spend time together begin to pick up each other's characteristics. This can happen between friends, relatives and married people. I had a friend with whom I lived for a period of time who, when she couldn't remember something, would talk about a 'doofus', particularly the remote control. After sharing a house for a while, I realized that I too was referring to a 'doofus'. I also had two friends who had been close friends for many years, and it was not unknown for them to turn up to an event in similar outfits.

Q: Have you ever noticed this experience or had it pointed out to you?

Introduction to disciple

The word *disciple* translates the Greek word *mathētés* (μαθητής), which refers to somebody who receives instruction from another. As mentioned above, the word means far more than a student

My thoughts and notes...

– it could be more akin to our word apprentice. It is so much more than just studying in a classroom; it is watching how things are done and trying to replicate it in the learner's life.

My thoughts and notes...

This was simple for the disciples while Jesus was there with them. But at the beginning of Acts, Jesus ascends into heaven and leaves them with no physical person to follow.

For the apostles and disciples this wasn't too much of a problem; they had been around Jesus long enough to follow him closely. They watched him, heard him and spent their lives living alongside him. After Pentecost when the Holy Spirit came on them they were also filled with the wisdom, power and presence of God within and with them.

However, what about the new converts who had never met Jesus? They had the Holy Spirit to guide them but they hadn't had the physical presence of the person of Jesus to follow. They had the Holy Spirit guiding them but didn't have an earthly model to help show them how following God could be lived out.

Wider body

The early Church was left with the question of how people who hadn't met or engaged with Jesus were to be discipled. This is an issue we also find ourselves with. The Holy Spirit is God's way of ensuring that we are equipped to follow him as he lives within us, but it is not the same experience that the disciples had of living alongside the physical body of Jesus.

Bible focus

Read Acts 16:1–5

[1] Paul came to Derbe and then to Lystra, where a disciple named Timothy lived, whose mother was Jewish and a believer but whose father was a Greek. [2] The believers at Lystra and Iconium spoke well of him. [3] Paul wanted to take him along on the journey, so he circumcised him because of the Jews who lived in that area, for they all knew that his father was a Greek. [4] As they traveled from town to town, they delivered the decisions reached by the apostles and elders in Jerusalem for the people to obey. [5] So the churches were strengthened in the faith and grew daily in numbers.

Q: What strikes you about this passage?

Q: What questions do you have?

The Church Unleashed as Disciple

On Paul's very first missionary journey, he headed through Lystra[7], where he prayed for a man lame from birth who was healed. He and Barnabas preached the gospel to the town before being stoned and left for dead. However, on the return leg of the journey, he returned to encourage the first beginnings of a church there.

Then on his second journey about three years later, he returned to find a more established community of Christians. One of the people he met was Timothy who may have witnessed, and certainly would have heard about Paul's miracle and persecution. Others in the community commend Timothy to Paul, who must've seen something in him because he invited him to come along with him.

Here, Paul was copying the example of Jesus – he was inviting a younger, less experienced follower to join him and be discipled. After that, Timothy travelled with Paul, was taught by him and lived alongside him. He was first Paul's disciple and then his constant companion and co-worker in preaching.

Q: What are the advantages of this type of intense personal discipleship?

Q: What are the challenges with it?

Although we often think of it as following a commitment, discipleship often starts before conversion. As we open up our everyday lives to the people around us, we allow them to find Jesus in both our lives and ourselves. They often encounter him through us first, before connecting with him for themselves.

However, as the Church, we are not always very good at continuing to disciple people once they come to faith.

Q: How does your church disciple those who are not yet Christian?

Q: How does your church disciple those who have made a commitment?

As a church, we have a tendency to want to give courses. This isn't to criticize any course in particular, but it's useful to remember that Jesus didn't ever give a course; he gave teaching sessions to large groups of people, but he engaged deeply with a few

---

Acts 14:8-10

closer ones.

Q: Why do you think that the Church is drawn to giving courses (there may be practical reasons for this)?

Q: What are some of the advantages and disadvantages to this model?

There are other ways of engaging with people and helping them to grow in their faith that don't involve attending a course. Some of this is about creating opportunities for people on the edges to experience the lives of those closer to Jesus. These may be formal or more informal, but they are ways of travelling alongside one another and going deeper in life.

Q: As a church community, what opportunities do you have for people to live alongside others and so to grow in faith?

Parts of the Body

Paul journeyed with Timothy in the model that Jesus demonstrated, which was a typical rabbinical method of discipleship. Students would typically travel around listening to the teaching of different rabbis and hearing their perspectives on certain issues before selecting one to follow. They would then soak themselves in the habits, teaching and lifestyle of their particular rabbi. Paul saw Timothy's potential and invited him to go along and be discipled by him.

We all fulfil both aspects of Paul and Timothy. We are all learners and disciples in our Christian journey – none of us, even the greatest scholars and holy people have arrived at a point where we live and understand everything that Jesus taught. In actual fact, often the more we know about God, the further away from him we can feel, similar to astrophysicists who, the more they understand about the universe, become aware of how much more there is to understand.

Q: If you imagine yourselves in the role of Timothy – who in the past has been your Paul? This may include Sunday school leaders, parents, church leaders or youth group leaders.

Q: What do you think about the fact that we never arrive? How does this make you feel?

Q: Who are you learning from now? Who is your Paul?

The reality is that in most of our churches, there are not enough people with enough time to disciple everyone that wants to be mentored.

We need to take responsibility for our own growth and learning, and if we are unable to access somebody to disciple us, we need to explore other options for us to grow. To stay the same is not an option for a disciple; a disciple by definition is somebody who is learning and growing.

What do you think about the ideas that we are always learning and that we need to take some responsibility for our own growth?

Q: What different ways can you think of that would allow you to grow and develop as Christians?

Some could include: reading books by modern authors, reading about the Church fathers and mothers and things they have written, attending conferences (like Spring Harvest), forming a prayer triplet to share life with others, studying the Bible alone, alongside commentaries or even in groups with others, finding a Spiritual Director to journey alongside you.

Q: How are you allowing yourself to be discipled?

Once we have accepted that we may be Timothy, we need to also consider the fact that we may be Paul too. Once we have started the journey of faith, there will always be others who are further back than us in the journey. If we are to 'do what Jesus did', then we need to consider the idea of being a discipler, sharing our life with a Timothy to help them to grow and develop. We don't need to have arrived in order to do that – we can still be journeying; we are just slightly further ahead on the journey than the ones we are travelling with.

Q: How do you feel about the idea of being a Paul?

Q: Who is your Timothy or who could your Timothy be?

Q: What are the advantages and disadvantages of this?

My thoughts and notes...

The Church Unleashed as Disciple 51

▶ Response

Reflect on your life and consider who has discipled you in the past and whom you've discipled. Fill them in and then thank God for those relationships.

Then prayerfully consider the future. Who is discipling or who might disciple you in the future and whom might you disciple? If you find it hard to put these names in, then commit to praying about it in the week ahead. Be aware of the Holy Spirit who may put certain people in your heart or across your path.

Pray for these people and the opportunities.

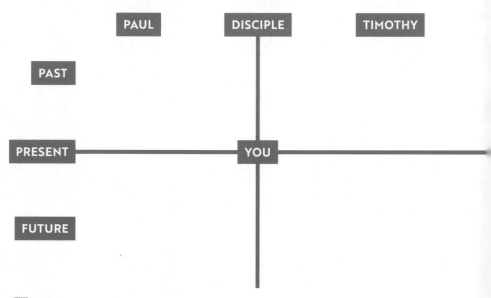

▶ Prayer

Thank you, God, for all those people who have shared their lives with mine, in a little or major way. Thank you for the example of Paul and Timothy in how to become a church that is a group of disciples learning and growing.

Father, please help us to continue to grow closer to you in what we think, what we do and what we say.

Father, we pray for those whose lives we influence and speak into; help us to model love, grace, forgiveness and perseverance that they may see you in us and grow in relationship with you themselves.

Lord, help us to be a church unleashed to disciple and be discipled.

In Jesus' name we pray,

Amen

oing Deeper

e main academic source for this Bible study was the work of Avery Dulles entitled
dels of The Church. It was originally written in 1978 and then revised in the 1980s but
till a key text that is used to study the Church.

alized that there may be those who would appreciate an opportunity to go slightly
eper and look at some quotes from the book itself, so I have compiled a list of
gestions for a group that is so inclined. The titles in brackets are Dulles' original
egories. There is also a more recent expanded version of the book that has its own
dy guide.

Church as Family (mystical communion)

he Community is constituted by the complete elf-forgetfulness of love. The relationship etween I and thou is no longer essentially a 'emanding but a giving one. [8]

What is this quote saying?

What would this look like in a church context?

What are the barriers to achieving this?

n many instances, the effort to find a perfect nterpersonal communion [community] in the 'hurch has led to frustration if not to apostasy. While the Church promises communion, it does ot always provide it in very evident form. 'hristians commonly experience the Church more s companionship of fellow travellers on the ame journey than as a union of lovers dwelling n the same home[9]

How true do you think this is?

What can the local church do to hold people's expectations and hopes of finding the 'perfect human community?'

> My thoughts and notes...

Dietrich Bonhoeffer The Communion of Saints (Dulles (2002) pg

Dulles (2002) pg 53

Church as Servant

The Church is the Church only when it exists for others. To make a start, it should give away all its property to those in need. The clergy must live solely on the free-will offerings of their congregations, or possibly engage in some secular calling. The Church must share in the secular problems of ordinary human life, not dominating, but helping and serving.[10]

- To what extent to do you agree with this quote?

- What are the problems and advantages of such a radical concept?

[Church as servant] reflects a consciousness of these needs of both the Church and the world. It seeks to give the Church a new relevance, a new vitality, a new modernity and a new sense of mission. The effort on the Church's part to overcome its pride, its corporate egoism and its callousness toward human misery promises to bring about a great spiritual renewal within the Church itself. Not only individual persons in the Church, but the Church itself, can be transformed into altruistic service toward the poor and the oppressed. This service can include prophetic criticism of social institutions and thus help to transform human society into the image of the promised Kingdom.[11]

- How would you sum this up?

- Does it make a difference if you consider it was written in the 1970s – do you think the author would still write the same?

- How has your church been transformed?

Church in Power

(This is in addition to Dulles' categories.)

Christian signs and wonders are beyond rationality, but they serve a rational purpose to authenticate the gospel. The gospel is opposed to the pluralistic lie that says all religious

---

10   D. Bonhoeffer *Letters and Papers from Prison*, rev. ed quoted in Dulles (2002) pg 87
11   Dulles (2002) pgs 90-91

experience is equally valid. Signs and wonders validate Christ's sacrifice on the cross and His lordship over every area of our lives.[12]

- How do signs and wonders point to Jesus?

- What is your understanding of the place of signs and wonders in the Church today? How does this compare to the early church?

Church as Herald

This mission [as herald] of the Church is one of proclamation of the Word of God to the whole world. The Church cannot hold itself responsible for the failure of [people] to accept it as God's Word, it has only to proclaim it with integrity and persistence. All else is secondary.[13]

'The Word of God and the Church are inseparable.'[14]

- To what extent do you agree with these quotes?

- How do we hold this in tension with the requirement to be heard and understood?

Church as sign (sacrament)

The Church is therefore is in the first instance a sign. It must signify in a historically tangible form the redeeming grace of Christ. It signifies that grace as relevantly given to [people] of every age, race kind, and condition. Hence the Church must incarnate itself in every human culture.

The Church does not always signify this equally well. It stands under a divine imperative to make itself a convincing sign. It appears most fully as a sign when its members are evidently united to one another and to God through holiness and mutual love and when they visibly gather to confess their faith in Christ and to celebrate what God has done for them in Christ.[15]

How does the 'Church incarnate itself in every human culture'?

Wimber and Springer (2009) pg137
Richard McBrien Church: The Continuing Quest (ibid pg 69)
R Bultmann Theology of the New Testament quoted in Dulles
)2) pg 72
Ibid., pg 60–61

- What changes in culture have you seen over the last 20 years, and how has the Church changed to incarnate itself in the new culture?
- Is there a tension in being incarnate in culture and a united holy group?

▶ Church as Disciple

As has been shown at some length in other studies, the various New Testament authors nuance the concept of discipleship in differing ways so as to address more effectively the situation of the particular communities for which they are writing. Mark . . . may be understood as giving special prominence to empowerment for Christian mission. Matthew gives special attention to initiation into the deeper significance of Jesus' teaching. Luke accents the breaking of old ties and total attachment to the person of Jesus. John stresses election to membership in a community sharply opposed to the 'world'. Paul emphasizes self-emptying love in imitation of Jesus.[16]

- Can you see evidence for the author's claims within the New Testament?
- If you were writing a letter, what aspects of discipleship would you want to emphasize to your church? your neighbourhood? society?

▶ Final discussion

Are there any other characteristics that you would like to add to the list?

---

16   Dulles (2002) pg 203

Bibliography

Avery S. J. Dulles, *Models of the Church*
John Wimber and Kevin Springer, *Power Evangelism*

The Church Unleashed as Family
Chris Green, *The Message of the Church*
Rob Suggs, *LifeBuilders: Christian Community*
Sim Denby, *Simply Church*

The Church Unleashed as Servant
Alan Scott, *Scattered Servants*
Freddie Pimm, *The Selfish Gospel*
R. Paul Stevens, *LifeBuilders: Service*)

The Church Unleashed in Power
J. I. Packer, *Keep in Step With the Spirit*
Simon Ponsonby, *More*
Mike Turrigiano and Luke Geraty, *I'm No Superhero*

The Church Unleashed as Herald
Phil Knox, *Story Bearer*
Rebecca Manley Pippert, *Out of the Saltshaker*
Rebecca Manley Pippert and Ruth Siemens, *LifeBuilders: Evangelism*

The Church Unleashed as Organization
Gerald L. Sittser, *Love One Another*
Douglas Connelly, *LifeBuilders: Seven Letters to Seven Churches*
John Stott, *The Church: A Unique Gathering of People*

The Church Unleashed as Sign
Graham Beynon, *God's New Community*
Neil Hudson, *Imagine Church*
Phyllis J. Le Peau, *LifeBuilders: Acts*

The Church Unleashed as Disciple
John Valentine, *Follow Me*
Fils Rogers, *Making Disciples*
James Bryan Smith, *The Good and Beautiful God*
Fils Rogers, *What if We Knew What God Knows About Us*